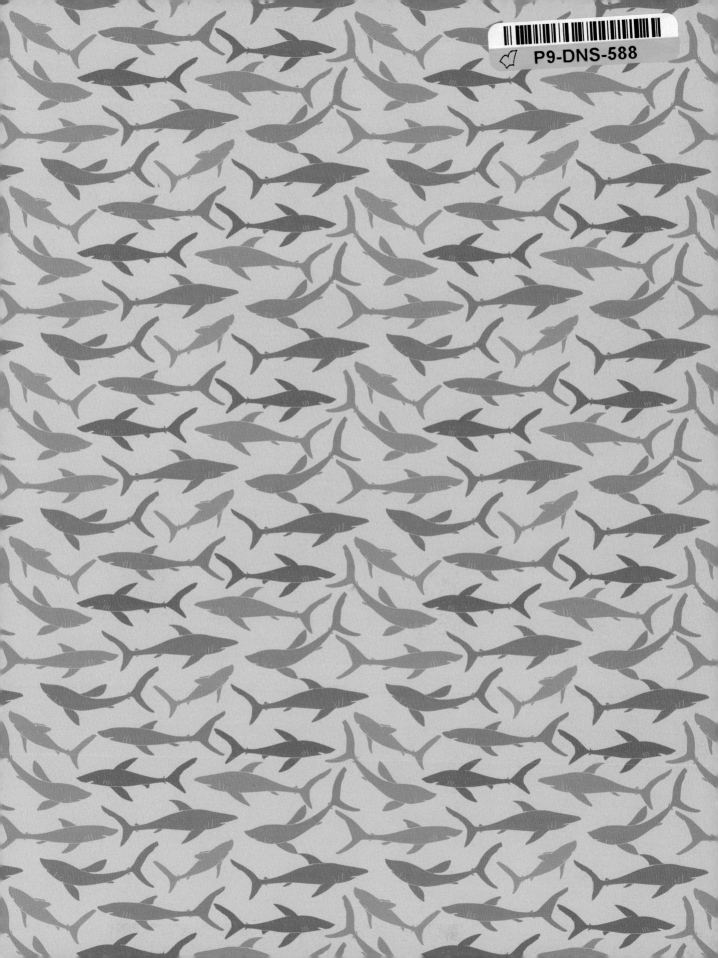

JOURNEY TO SHARK ISLAND:
A SHARK PHOTOGRAPHER'S CLOSE ENCOUNTERS

by Mary M. Cerullo

Photographs by Jeffrey L. Rotman

Consultant: James Sulikowski, PhD
Marine Science Department, University of New England

COMPASS POINT BOOKS
a capstone imprint

Compass Point Books are published by Capstone,
1710 Roe Crest Drive, North Mankato, Minnesota 56003
www.capstonepub.com

Editorial Credits
Kristen Mohn, editor; Veronica Scott, designer; Svetlana Zhurkin, media researcher;
Tori Abraham, production specialist

Photo Credits
All photographs by Jeffrey L. Rotman with the exception of:
Adam Rotman, 12; Asher Gal, 1 (bottom), 25; Avi Klapfer, 5; Isabelle Delafosse, 3, 40 (right);
Shutterstock: Leonardo Gonzalez, 24, Sergey Dubrov, 9 (bottom)
Design Elements by Shutterstock

Library of Congress Cataloging-in-Publication Data
Cerullo, Mary M., author.
  Journey to shark island : a shark photographer's close encounters / By Mary M. Cerullo ;
Photographs by Jeffrey L. Rotman.
     pages cm. — (Compass point books. Shark expedition)
  Summary: "Provides information on sharks and shares a shark diver's experiences on Cocos
Island, Costa Rica"— Provided by publisher.
Includes index.
  ISBN 978-0-7565-4887-2 (library binding)
  ISBN 978-0-7565-4910-7 (paperback)
  ISBN 978-0-7565-4914-5 (eBook PDF)
1. Rotman, Jeffrey L.—Juvenile literature. 2. Sharks—Pacific Ocean—Juvenile literature.
3. Sharks—Costa Rica—Cocos Island—Juvenile literature. 4. Wildlife photographers—Juvenile
literature. 5. Underwater photography—Juvenile literature. 6. Cocos Island (Costa Rica)—Juvenile
literature. I. Rotman, Jeffrey L., photographer. II. Title.
TR729.F5C47 2015
597.309164'2—dc23   2014008678

To Meg & Erik, wishing you excitement on all your expeditions,
  above and below the waves—MMC
For Oren, a man of the sea—JLR

Printed in the United States of America in
North Mankato, Minnesota
032014   008087CGF14

TABLE OF CONTENTS

COCOS ISLAND 4

HUNTING HAMMERHEADS 14

SILVERTIPS BY DAY 18

WHITETIPS AT NIGHT 20

TIGER SHARKS TAKE OVER 22

SURROUNDED BY SILKY SHARKS 24

PROTECTING THE CREATURES
OF SHARK ISLAND 30

GLOSSARY 38

READ MORE 39

INTERNET SITES 39

INDEX 40

COCOS ISLAND

The diver plunged into the ocean, kicked his long swim fins, and headed straight down the side of the jagged cliff of an extinct volcano. He passed by a colorful school of fairy basslets. A spiny lobster peeked out from its hiding place in the black rock.

At 100 to 130 feet (30 to 40 meters), where the sunlight is only a distant glow, underwater photographer Jeff Rotman spotted his prey. He dove even deeper to get underneath the school of fish for the best shot of the giant creatures. Jeff raised his camera and clicked photo after photo before the 100 scalloped hammerhead sharks dispersed in fright, terrified by the flash of his camera.

Jeff had come thousands of miles to Cocos Island to get just this image.

Scalloped hammerheads have a distinctive shape that makes them instantly recognizable.

Costa Rica's Cocos Island is a tiny volcanic island in the Pacific Ocean, far from any place inhabited by humans. Over the years Jeff has visited Cocos Island many times. He has seen firsthand that many of the shark species that were once plentiful there have all but disappeared because of overfishing. Now Jeff comes not just to photograph the sharks, but also to document the dangers that threaten them. He hopes his photos can show why it's so important to protect the top predators of the ocean.

SHARK CENTRAL

To underwater explorers like Jeff, Cocos Island is known as the Island of the Sharks. In addition to sea turtles, whales, and dolphins, the waters surrounding Cocos Island have manta rays, tiger sharks, hammerhead sharks, whale sharks, and many more kinds of sharks rarely seen in other places—and never in the huge numbers found here. "Cocos Island is the single best place on the planet to see a variety of sharks," Jeff says.

But Cocos Island isn't easy to get to. It's more than 300 miles (500 kilometers) off the coast of Central America. Jeff travels on the dive boat *Sea Hunter* out of Costa Rica. It takes 45 hours of bouncing over rough seas to reach the island.

The island and the waters for 9 miles (15 km) around it make up the Cocos Island National Park. The park has rules for visitors; for example, only three boats have permission to take divers to visit the underwater park, and only the park ranger may stay overnight on Cocos Island. So the 90-foot- (27-m-) long dive boat is Jeff's home for the next 30 days.

AT SEA ON *SEA HUNTER*

The *Sea Hunter* is not luxurious. It is a workboat that was formerly a scientific research vessel. Divers share cramped quarters with four bunks in each cabin. Most of the rest of the space is filled with scuba tanks and other diving equipment, storage lockers, and workstations for doing research or viewing film footage.

a bigeye thresher shark at Cocos Island

So what is it about Cocos Island that makes it Shark Central? Food, of course. You might say it's like a giant seafood buffet—an all-you-can-eat feast for sharks.

Several ocean currents swirl around the island. Where ocean currents converge, marine life gathers. Ocean currents are often called "ocean highways." They transport tiny plants and animals called plankton, which directly or indirectly feed almost everything else in the ocean.

Larger ocean creatures, such as turtles, whales, and fish, converge as they follow the currents or are swept up by them, until they reach the rich feeding grounds of Cocos Island. Scientists say there are about 300 different species of fish that live around Cocos Island. Wherever there are small fish, bigger ones, such as sharks, come too.

Many sharks also visit the area for another reason—the presence of many different kinds of cleaner fish. Big fish gather at cleaning stations on the coral reef to wait for the cleaners to work on them. Cleaner fish perform a useful service by plucking annoying parasites off the skin, gills, and jaws of the larger fish. The sharks get cleaned, and the little cleaners get a meal.

A trumpetfish hides among a school of blue-striped snappers.

STAYING SAFE IN STRONG CURRENTS

Exploring the deep, treacherous waters of Cocos Island is only for experienced divers. The currents are so strong that they can carry divers far away from their dive boats. To make sure he isn't lost at sea, Jeff carries a long orange rubber tube that he can blow up should he get swept away by the current. In such circumstances, he'd wave it in the air so that the dive boat could find him. For night dives he packs a strobe light, like a bicycle rider might use. If needed, the flashing light would signal his location.

9

TRICKS OF THE TRADE

It's one thing to see a shark; it's quite another to shoot the perfect photograph of one. Jeff Rotman has learned many strategies to make the most of his dive expeditions.

1. FIND A SHARK.

This is the first challenge. Jeff has used high-tech tools including spotter planes to locate whale sharks. Other times his tools are as simple as a cut-out figure of a seal, like the duck decoys used by hunters. The seal silhouette prompted a great white shark to leap out of the water right next to Jeff—a dream shot for a shark photographer.

2. OFFER TREATS.

Food is a good way to introduce yourself to a shark or ray, says Jeff. Chum, a tasty mixture of horsemeat, blood, and fish oil, is a yummy draw for great whites. But be careful—too many treats can get your subject overexcited.

3. SAFETY FIRST.

No matter how eager he is to get his shot, Jeff always takes safety measures. Sometimes he wears a chainmail dive suit. That works for medium-sized sharks like Caribbean reef sharks, but only a strong shark cage provides enough protection when you are diving among great whites.

4. BRING A BUDDY.

Jeff always has another diver to watch his back—literally. He never dives anywhere without his safety diver and good friend, Asher Gal.

5. BE POLITE.

Jeff says that this is the most important rule of diving with sharks. You are a guest in their world. Don't chase, corner, or grab them. Let them come to you. Or, if you are Jeff, inch toward them very, very slowly.

tiger shark

Jeff shooting Caribbean reef sharks

THINKING LIKE A SHARK

Jeff's job begins long before he jumps into the water with his camera. Before any dive expedition, he does his homework, learning all he can about the kinds of sharks he may meet. He tries to understand and predict how they will behave around him.

Although Jeff has a checklist of the animals he hopes to photograph on his trips to Cocos Island, he is prepared for whatever shows up at this crossroads in the Pacific Ocean. He hopes to find schools of scalloped hammerheads, silky sharks, whitetip and silvertip sharks, and even dangerous tiger sharks. But swordfish, sailfish, tuna, whale sharks, Galápagos sharks, and many more large fish also come here, where nutritious tidbits are pushed up from the deep, supplying food for all.

When Jeff (right) and Asher Gal are working in remote areas like Cocos Island, they have to bring 10 to 12 different cameras and back-up gear for everything. There are no stores to resupply.

Jeff photographs Asher with a swordfish being illegally caught by fishermen. Jeff uses his photos to let the world know what is happening to the ocean's top predators.

HUNTING HAMMERHEADS

It's not hard to figure out how the hammerhead shark got its name—its head is shaped like a hammer. At either end of its flattened head sit its eyes and nostrils. A hammerhead swings its head from side to side as it swims. Having eyes at either end of that broad head may help it scan a wider area on the ocean floor as it searches for prey.

Around its nose, mouth, and jaws are many tiny pores called ampullae of Lorenzini. They are the source of the shark's amazing ability to detect the electricity given off by other animals, such as a stingray buried in the sand. Scientists say the shark uses its head to pin the stingray down before grasping it with razor-sharp teeth. Many hammerheads have a stingray spine embedded in their jaws to prove it.

With eyes on either side, a hammerhead has a head made for hunting.

SCALLOPED HAMMERHEAD STATS

AVERAGE SIZE
10 to 12 feet (3 to 3.7 m)

MAXIMUM SIZE
14 feet (4.3 m)

MAXIMUM WEIGHT
336 pounds (152 kilograms)

RANGE
tropical Atlantic and Pacific oceans

LIFE SPAN
more than 30 years

DIET
mostly fish, small stingrays, sardines,
mackerel, and herring

FACT:

Scalloped hammerheads can be huge and scary-looking, but they are actually rather shy around divers. Scalloped hammerheads are not dangerous man-eaters like the infamous great hammerhead.

Jeff waited hours to capture this shot of a scalloped hammerhead waiting its turn to be groomed at a cleaning station.

Jeff was on a mission to photograph hammerheads. The dive boat operators took him to a cove where scalloped hammerheads come to get groomed by cleaner fish. Jeff dove to a depth of about 100 feet (30 m) and squatted down on the ocean floor behind a big rock. For several minutes he sat motionless, his camera at the ready, making himself part of the landscape. Jeff's safety diver, Asher, stood guard a short distance away. They watched and waited for the hammerheads to arrive.

Their patience was rewarded when a giant school of 100 scalloped hammerheads swam past them. One turned off from the group and headed toward a big boulder where cleaner fish waited—and where Jeff was hiding. When the shark neared the cleaning station, it slowed almost to a standstill to let small cleaner fish called barberfish do their job. Jeff got several shots before the camera-shy hammerhead turned and fled.

"DEEPSEE" DIVING

To find scalloped hammerheads in deeper water, Jeff boarded the *DeepSee*, a submersible that can carry three people to a depth of 1,500 feet (450 m). *DeepSee*'s thick acrylic sphere provides a 360-degree view so it feels like you are actually swimming among the fish, even though you are at a depth that would crush a diver.

The crew descended along the steep slope of the extinct volcano. At 500 feet (150 m), it was so dark that the lights of the submersible didn't reach more than 25 feet (7.6 m). A scalloped hammerhead materialized out of the gloom and nearly crashed into the submersible. "It was a lovely surprise," remembers Jeff. "Being surprised is one of the things you can always count on at Cocos."

SILVERTIPS BY DAY

Other sharks congregated at various cleaning stations on the ocean floor. Jeff's dive guides showed him a shallow cove where every afternoon around 3:30 p.m. silvertip sharks come to a cleaning station staffed by fish called trevally jacks. Each day the sharks would stay for an hour or more before swimming off into the sunset. The divers had never heard of this behavior in silvertips.

For eight days the divers watched in amazement as young and old silvertips repeated the ritual of stopping at this spot to be cleaned. Usually four to seven sharks showed up, always in the late afternoon. One of the biggest silvertips, about 8 feet (2.5 m) long, had a ragged lower jaw, a clue that it had made a narrow escape from a fishhook.

Silvertips can be dangerous if divers meet them in the open ocean. But here they usually ignored Jeff, who could creep up within several feet of them to get some shots. If he came any closer, though, the adult sharks would charge and swerve away at the last minute. "I crossed an invisible line. It was a clear message to me to back off! But after all," admits Jeff, "this is their territory."

SILVERTIP SHARK STATS

MAXIMUM SIZE
10 feet (3 m)

RANGE
tropical Indian and Pacific oceans

DIET
bony fish, eagle rays, and smaller sharks

WHITETIPS AT NIGHT

During the day Jeff explored shallow caves about 40 feet (12 m) below the surface, where many young whitetip reef sharks hang out, lounging on top of one another. At only 1.5 feet (46 cm) long, they hide in the rocks to avoid larger sharks that could easily gobble them up.

But the real adventure begins at night, when the adult whitetips go on the prowl. Like packs of wolves, they hunt and corner their prey. If one whitetip detects a sleeping parrotfish or surgeonfish inside a crack in the volcanic rock, the shark will try to force its snout into the hole to grab the fish. As the shark wriggles its whole body vigorously to try to reach the prey, its thrashing attracts as many as 50 other whitetips. They bombard the fish's hiding place until one of the sharks captures it. Then the other sharks often gang up on the winner to try to snatch its prize right out of its mouth.

FACT:

To make sure he disrupted the sharks' night behavior as little as possible, Jeff would let the batteries for his dive light run low during the day. Instead of a bright beam, it emitted only a faint glow, just enough for Jeff to find his way in the dark.

WHITETIP REEF SHARK STATS

AVERAGE SIZE
5 feet (1.5 m)

LIFE SPAN
16 to 20 years

MAXIMUM SIZE
6 feet (1.8 m)

DIET
fish, spiny lobsters, crabs,
and octopuses

RANGE
tropical Indian and Pacific oceans

Many whitetip reef sharks swarm around rocks where they know smaller fish are hiding.

TIGER SHARKS TAKE OVER

Scientists say the reason there are so many whitetip reef sharks at Cocos Island is that many larger sharks that would normally feed on the smaller sharks are gone—caught by fishermen. Without large predators, the population of whitetips has exploded.

Tiger sharks, famous for eating almost anything, have moved in to take advantage of the feast. The tiger sharks come into the shallow waters around Cocos Island at night to feed on whitetips, helping to reduce their population.

Sharks eat other sharks. Tiger sharks come to Cocos Island to feed on the smaller whitetip sharks.

TIGER TAMING

Like most sharks, a tiger shark is naturally curious about the funny, finned creatures that make lots of bubbles. Jeff's safety diver, Asher, carries a pole with three needlelike projections on one end. Just before a shark's curiosity prompts it to take a test bite, Asher gently taps the shark's snout with the pole. The shark quickly gets the message and backs off. Jeff says, "A test bite is one way that a shark can figure out if something is OK to eat. But I'd rather not be tested!"

Tiger sharks are among a handful of sharks that Jeff considers very dangerous. "I would never let a tiger shark out of my sight," he says. If he were attacked, as a last resort he would pull off his air tank and hold it in front of his chest to defend himself. So far, he has never had to.

TIGER SHARK STATS

AVERAGE SIZE
12 to 14 feet (3.7 to 4.3 m)

RANGE
worldwide in warm seas

LIFE SPAN
40 to 50 years

DIET
marine mammals, marine reptiles, fish, lobsters, and squid

FACT:

Besides eating other sharks, tiger sharks feed on stingrays, seals, birds, and squid. Occasionally, they also munch on stranger fare. Car license plates, alarm clocks, bricks, bottles, and beer cans have been found inside the stomachs of tiger sharks, earning them the nickname "swimming trashcans."

SURROUNDED BY SILKY SHARKS

One way Jeff locates sharks is by watching what other animals do. Where lots of animals gather, you know there's something exciting going on.

Jeff really wanted to photograph a phenomenon called a bait ball, in which sharks feed mid-ocean on a huge school of fish. Bait balls occur when a school of fish is squeezed into a tight circle by predators both below and above. Sharks, dolphins, or tuna force the school to the surface, where seabirds join the attack from the air. It's a feeding frenzy photo opportunity. And it's a very, very dangerous place to be.

Jeff spent hours each day at Cocos scanning the horizon with his binoculars. He was on the lookout for seabirds shrieking and diving into the water. After six days of waiting, he saw a commotion not far away. Jeff and the dive team jumped into their inflatable boat and raced to the site where frigate birds and brown-footed boobies were gorging themselves. Some were already too heavy to fly. They paddled around weakly, their bellies stuffed with fish called green jacks.

bait ball

Diving birds signal action
just below the surface.

Jeff and Asher dove into the water about 200 feet (60 m) from the bait ball. It was already late afternoon, and the approaching sunset made it harder for the divers to see very far underwater. Within seconds, dozens of silky sharks swarmed around them. As the feeding continued, the sharks became more and more excited. Jeff tried to focus his camera as Asher stayed nearby with extra cameras at the ready.

The light was too dim for Jeff to get a good shot without using the flash on his camera. When he turned on his strobe light, the high-pitched whine of the battery made the sharks go wild. They began to ram the divers with their snouts. It felt like being punched in the stomach. Jeff and Asher looked at each other through their masks and were of the same mind: It was time to get out of there.

They kicked to the surface and flagged down the waiting boat. As they flopped into it, they agreed that there must be more than 100 silkies below them. It was only then that they could admire how the light had shimmered against the silky skin that these sharks were named for.

Even though it's shiny, the skin of silkies is as tough as any other shark's

SILKY SHARK STATS

AVERAGE SIZE
7 to 8 feet (2.1 to 2.4 m)

MAXIMUM SIZE
10 feet (3 m)

RANGE
warm waters of the Atlantic,
Pacific, and Indian oceans

LIFE SPAN
more than 20 years

DIET
tuna, small fish, squid, and crabs

NICKNAME
net-eater, because it often tears up seine nets
set out to catch tuna

Suddenly, the water around the boat began to boil with jumping fish frantic to escape the sharks. Four jacks landed in the boat. Then there was a huge POW! Sharks were ramming the hard underside of the raft.

The boat had drifted directly over the bait ball, and the small fish were trying desperately to hide beneath it. For 20 minutes sharks slammed into the bottom of the boat, trying to catch the fish cowering there. Only the wooden planks on the floor of the boat separated the sharks from the crew.

More small fish tried to escape by leaping out of the water. Then the divers saw an amazing sight—a silky shark bolted right out of the water, its mouth crammed with fish.

Finally the sun disappeared below the horizon. Ten minutes later, the water around them was quiet. Only gentle waves rocked the boat. The sharks were gone—but not forgotten. It was the closest that Jeff and Asher had ever come to being shark bait.

PROTECTING THE CREATURES OF SHARK ISLAND

Many sharks swim great distances across the world's oceans yet return regularly to a home base, a place such as Costa Rica's Cocos Island. The waters around Cocos Island provide a sanctuary where sharks are supposed to be safe. It is illegal for sharks to be caught by fishermen within the national park. Where sharks are protected, they usually live long enough to have young so that there will be more sharks in the future.

Jeff has visited Cocos Island many times in the past 15 years. Over that time he has seen the number and size of the sharks shrink, devastated by illegal fishing. Some species have been fished out altogether.

a young blacktip shark hooked on a longline

Jeff has made friends with fishermen who work near the protected waters around Cocos Island. He's lived aboard their boats for weeks at a time, filming the fishing practice of longlining in order to make the public aware of what's happening. Fishermen roll out miles of fishing line late in the afternoon and haul them back into the boat at sunrise. With as many as 2,000 baited hooks, longlines are meant to catch legal fish such as tuna. But they often snare unintended creatures as well, such as seabirds, sea turtles, and sharks.

Asher attempts to remove a fishhook from a caught sea turtle. Sea turtles are protected from being hunted in Cocos Island National Park.

Jeff uses his skills as a photographer
to try to save sharks.

Some longline fishermen, like those around Cocos Island, specifically target sharks. These fishermen might stay out for three weeks at a time. Their small boats have little room to store their catch and no ice to keep it fresh. So they cut off the fins to sell and toss what's left of the maimed sharks overboard.

Unable to swim without their fins, the injured sharks sink and die a slow death.

Fishing for sharks is illegal within the boundaries of Cocos Island National Park. But Jeff says that it is only in the last 10 years that environmental laws meant to protect sharks there have been enforced.

SHARK FIN SOUP

In most seas of the world, sharks are captured specifically for their fins. The fins may be sold for as much as $600 a pound for shark fin soup, a delicacy in some Asian cultures. At a cost of $65 to $150 a bowl, the soup usually is served only on special occasions.

An estimated 26 million to 73 million sharks are killed every year to meet the demand for shark fin soup. It's hard to imagine 73 million of anything. Think of it this way: The 2012 U.S. census found that the entire population of people under the age of 18 in the United States numbered about 73 million. It's a big number.

Jeff has spent many hours in places around the world filming the gruesome results of shark finning in order to help stop the practice. Jeff's photographs have told the story in publications in more than 25 countries. Environmental organizations working on conservation campaigns use the photos to educate people about what is happening to sharks. This effort is helping to make a difference, as people realize the harm that eating shark fin soup is doing to the ocean's top predators. More places, including the United States, China, and Hong Kong, are passing laws to stop the sale of shark fin soup. Shark finning is being banned in many countries.

If these laws are enforced, there may still be a future for sharks.

Shark watchers spend hundreds of millions of dollars a year on dive trips to swim with sharks, but those who make money from ecotourism usually are not the same people who fish for sharks.

If people can help local fishermen earn more money by keeping sharks alive for tourism than they can make killing them for soup, there may still be a future for sharks.

One of the main reasons Jeff travels the world photographing sharks is to show how awesome they are. Sharks don't have the "cute" appeal dolphins or seals have, but they need protecting just as much. Without sharks, sick animals would spread disease, injured fish would suffer longer, and decaying carcasses would litter the ocean and wash up on shore.

If everyone stops viewing sharks as sea monsters and instead learns more about the important role they serve in our oceans, there may still be a future for sharks.

As painful as it is to see a shark without its fins, Jeff hopes his photographs will motivate people to help stop the cruel practice of finning.

THE FUTURE FOR SHARKS

About 400 to 450 different kinds of sharks have been discovered so far, and Jeff Rotman has photographed around 100 of them. When Jeff looks back over his career as an underwater photographer, he says, "The ocean is a different place from the one in which I started diving 40 years ago. It will never be the same again, but with the help of people who care about the ocean, who want to see sharks and other sea creatures thrive, perhaps it will be wonderful still."

Jeff Rotman is where he loves to be— surrounded by sharks.

GLOSSARY

ampullae of Lorenzini—pores on the snouts of sharks and rays containing sensors that detect weak electric currents

bait ball—a tight school of fish formed when the fish crowd together as they are attacked by predators from above and below

chum—food dropped into the water to lure sharks; chum is often made up of dead fish parts

cleaner fish—a small fish, often with a distinctive stripe, that identifies itself as an animal that picks off parasites and dead skin from larger fish

cleaning station—an area on the ocean floor where fish gather to be cleaned of parasites

ecotourism—visiting a place that has unspoiled natural resources, while being careful to have minimal impact on the environment

extinct—no longer living; an extinct volcano is one that will not erupt again

finning—the practice of cutting off a shark's fins and discarding the shark, often still alive, back into the ocean

parasite—an organism that lives on or in another organism in order to get nourishment or protection

plankton—single-celled plants and animals that drift with currents

scuba—self-contained underwater breathing apparatus, based on the device developed by Emile Gagnan and Jacques Cousteau, which uses a tank of compressed gas (usually air) for diving

submersible—a small vessel used underwater, usually for research

READ MORE

Discovery Channel. *The Big Book of Sharks.*
New York: Time Home Entertainment, 2012.

Lourie, Peter. *First Dive to Shark Dive.*
Honsdale, Pa.: Boyds Mills Press, 2009.

Simon, Seymour. *Seymour Simon's Extreme Oceans.*
San Francisco: Chronicle Books, 2013.

BEACH 50m →

INTERNET SITES

Use FactHound to find Internet sites related to this book.
All of the sites on FactHound have been researched by our staff.

Here's all you do:

Visit *www.facthound.com*

Type in this code:
9780756548872

AUTHOR

Mary M. Cerullo has been teaching and writing about the ocean and natural history for 40 years. She has written more than 20 children's books on ocean life. Mary is also associate director of the conservation organization Friends of Casco Bay/Casco Baykeeper in Maine, where she lives with her family.

Mary with granddaughter Taylor

PHOTOGRAPHER

Jeffrey L. Rotman is one of the world's leading underwater photographers. Diving and shooting for more than 40 years—and in nearly every ocean and sea in the world—this Boston native combines an artist's eye with a naturalist's knowledge of his subjects. His photography has been featured on television and in print worldwide. Jeff and his family live in New Jersey.

Jeff with sons Matthew and Thomas

INDEX

bait balls, 24, 26, 28–29

Caribbean reef sharks, 10, 11

cleaning stations, 8, 16, 17, 18

Cocos Island National Park, 6, 30, 31, 33

conservation, 5, 13, 30–36

Costa Rica, 5, 6, 30

currents, 8, 9

DeepSee submersible, 17

diving, 4, 7, 9, 10, 12, 17, 18, 20, 23, 26, 34

equipment, 7, 12, 23, 26

finning, 33–35

Gal, Asher, 10, 12, 13, 17, 23, 26, 29, 31

great white sharks, 10

hammerheads, scalloped, 4, 6, 12, 14–17

hunting, 10, 14, 20, 31

illegal fishing, 13, 22, 30, 33

longlining, 30, 33

prey, 14, 20, 21, 23

safety, 9, 10, 17, 23

seabirds, 23–25, 30

Sea Hunter, 8

sea turtles, 6, 8, 30, 31

silky sharks, 12, 26–29

silvertip sharks, 12, 18–19

swordfish, 12, 13

tiger sharks, 6, 11, 12, 22–23

whitetip sharks, 12, 20–21, 22

BEACH 50m

SURF

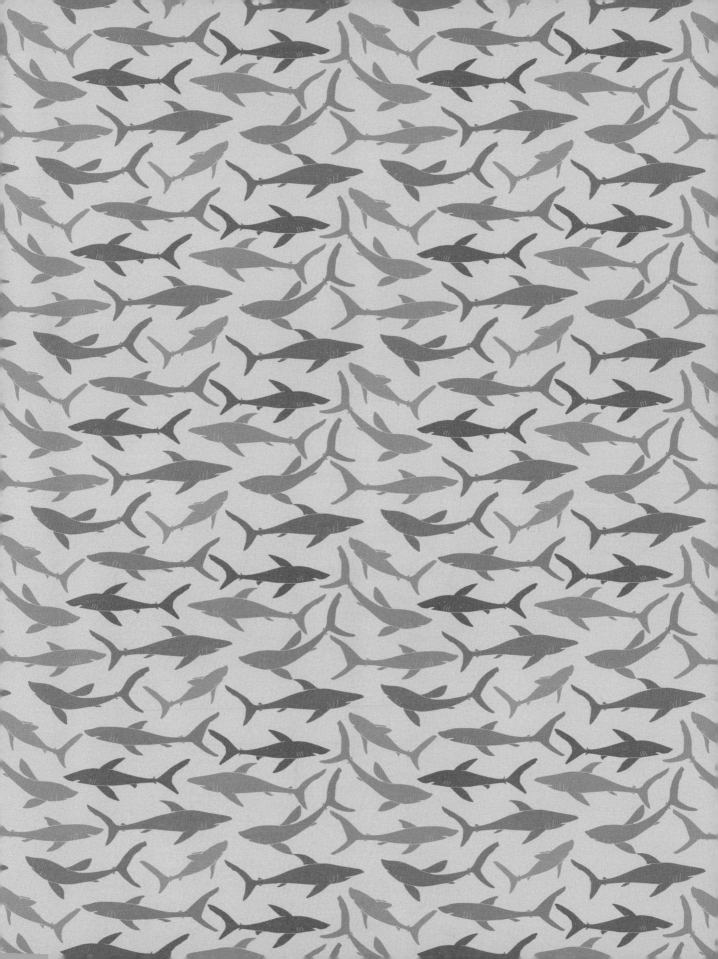